2024 NBA Predictions

By *Mike Bhangu*

BBP Copyright 2024

Copyright © 2024 by Mike Bhangu.

This book is licensed and is being offered for your personal enjoyment only. It is prohibited for this book to be re-sold, shared and/or to be given away to other people. If you would like to provide and/or share this book with someone else, please purchase an additional copy. If you did not personally purchase this book for your own personal enjoyment and are reading it, please respect the hard work of this author and purchase a copy for yourself.

All rights reserved. No part of this book may be used or reproduced or transmitted in any manner whatsoever without written permission from the author, except for the inclusion of brief quotations in reviews, articles, and recommendations. Thank you for honoring this.

_____

Published by BB Productions
British Columbia, Canada
thinkingmanmike@gmail.com

2024 NBA Predictions

Table of Contents

Chapter 1: Introduction
- Overview: The purpose of this analysis is to predict the winner of the 2024 NBA playoffs and the reasons for such prediction.

- Methodology: Explain the data and methods used to make the predictions, including consideration of current odds, team analysis, and external factors.

Chapter 2: Eastern Conference Contenders
- *Boston Celtics*
    - Strengths: Strong core duo, excellent coaching, depth and experience, strong defense, Damian Lillard's offensive boost.
    - Weaknesses: Potential for complacency, dependence on key players.

- *Milwaukee Bucks*
    - Strengths: Giannis Antetokounmpo's dominance, Jrue Holiday's two-way play, Khris Middleton's scoring threat, championship experience.
    - Weaknesses: Ageing core, reliance on Giannis, potential injury concerns.

- *Other Eastern Conference threats*
    - Briefly discuss potential contenders like Philadelphia 76ers, Miami Heat, or Cleveland Cavaliers.

Chapter 3: Western Conference Contenders

- *Denver Nuggets*
    - Strengths: Nikola Jokic's MVP potential, healthy Murray and Porter Jr., strong supporting cast, depth and versatility.
    - Weaknesses: Inexperienced backcourt, potential defensive struggles against elite teams.

- *Phoenix Suns*
    - Strengths: Devin Booker's scoring prowess, Chris Paul's leadership and playmaking, Deandre Ayton's dominance, strong team culture.
    - Weaknesses: Ageing Chris Paul, potential reliance on Booker, lack of size in the frontcourt.

- *Other Western Conference threats*
    - Briefly discuss potential contenders like Golden State Warriors, Los Angeles Clippers, or Los Angeles Lakers.

Chapter 4: Predicting the Conference Finals

- *Eastern Conference*
    - Analyze the potential matchups and predict the winner of the Eastern Conference Finals, justifying the decision

based on strengths and weaknesses of the remaining teams.

- *Western Conference*
  - Analyze the potential matchups and predict the winner of the Western Conference Finals, justifying the decision based on strengths and weaknesses of the remaining teams.

Chapter 5: NBA Finals Showdown

- *Prediction*
  - Based on the analysis in previous chapters, predict the winner of the NBA Finals and provide a detailed explanation for the choice.

- *Reasons*
  - Explain why the chosen team is favored to win the championship, considering factors like team balance, individual star power, coaching, and momentum.

- *Contingency Plans*
  - Discuss potential scenarios that could impact the prediction, such as injuries, unexpected upsets, or unexpected player performance.

Chapter 6: Conclusion and Disclaimers

- Recap the main points of the analysis and reiterate the predicted winner of the NBA championship.

- Acknowledge the limitations of predictions and emphasize the unpredictable nature of the playoffs.

Chapter 7: A Legacy Forged in Hardwood

Chapter 1: Introduction

This analysis delves into the exciting world of the 2024 NBA playoffs, aiming to predict the ultimate victor. By analyzing team strengths and weaknesses, current performance, and external factors, we embark on a journey to uncover the most likely contenders for the ultimate prize.

The Methodology of Prediction

Predicting the NBA championship winner is no easy feat. Multiple factors intertwine to create a complex tapestry of potential outcomes. To navigate this intricate landscape, this analysis employs a multi-faceted approach.

1. Current NBA Finals Odds:

The NBA Finals odds, as determined by reputable sportsbooks, serve as a valuable starting point. These odds reflect the collective judgment of experts and encapsulate the general expectations for each team's performance.

2. Team Analysis:

A comprehensive analysis of each team's performance throughout the regular season is crucial. This involves examining key statistics, offensive and defensive schemes, player strengths and weaknesses, and coaching philosophies. Identifying trends, patterns, and areas of improvement paints a vivid picture of each team's capabilities.

3. External Factors:

External factors beyond the control of teams can significantly influence playoff outcomes. These include injuries, trades, coaching changes, and home-court advantage. Careful consideration of these factors allows for a more nuanced and realistic prediction.

4. Historical Context:

Examining historical trends in the NBA playoffs offers valuable insights. Analyzing past championship winners, playoff upsets, and dominant performances helps to identify patterns and potential trends that might play out in the 2024 playoffs.

5. Expert Opinions:

Consulting the insights and predictions of renowned basketball analysts, journalists, and former players provides additional perspective. By incorporating their expertise, the analysis gains a broader and more informed view of the potential playoff landscape.

The Power of Prediction

Predicting the NBA championship winner is not merely an exercise in speculation. It serves several critical purposes.

1. Enhancing Fan Engagement:

Predicting the champion fuels the excitement and anticipation surrounding the playoffs. By engaging in discussions and debates, fans become more invested in the games, creating a vibrant and interactive community.

2. Sharpening Analytical Skills:
The process of analyzing teams, evaluating statistics, and considering external factors hones critical thinking skills and analytical abilities. By applying these skills to sports, individuals can develop a deeper understanding of the game and its nuances.

3. Fostering a Culture of Debate and Discussion:
Predictions spark spirited debates and healthy disagreements among fans. These discussions encourage individuals to articulate their arguments, defend their positions, and consider different perspectives. This fosters a culture of open dialogue and intellectual engagement.

4. Highlighting Team Strengths and Weaknesses:
Analyzing teams and predicting the champion shines a spotlight on their strengths and weaknesses. This allows fans to appreciate the unique skills and abilities of each player and team, while also fostering an understanding of areas that require improvement.

5. Preparing for the Unexpected:
While predictions strive for accuracy, the unpredictable nature of sports ensures that surprises and upsets are always possible. By contemplating different scenarios and potential outcomes, fans can be better prepared for the unexpected twists and turns that the playoffs inevitably bring.

Embracing the Journey

As we embark on this journey to predict the 2024 NBA champion, it's important to remember the inherent beauty of the playoffs. It's a time for celebration, passion, and the pursuit of sporting excellence. Regardless of the outcome, the playoffs offer a spectacle of talent, dedication, and the captivating drama of athletic competition.

With excitement buzzing and anticipation rising, we turn the page to Chapter 2, where we delve into the Eastern Conference contenders vying for the right to represent their division in the NBA Finals.

Chapter 2: Eastern Conference Contenders

The Eastern Conference of the NBA boasts a dynamic landscape of talented teams, each with their own distinct strengths, weaknesses, and aspirations. As the playoffs approach, the intensity of competition escalates, amplifying the stakes and showcasing the very best of basketball. Let's delve into the top contenders in the Eastern Conference, analyzing their capabilities and potential paths to the NBA Finals.

1. Boston Celtics
Strengths.

- A. Dynamic Duo: The Celtics possess a potent offensive core in Jayson Tatum and Jaylen Brown, two young stars who have blossomed into All-Star caliber players. Their versatility, scoring prowess, and defensive tenacity make them a formidable duo.

- B. Coaching Prowess: Joe Mazzulla has seamlessly transitioned into the head coaching role, demonstrating a keen understanding of the team and its strengths. His tactical adjustments and ability to motivate players have been instrumental in the Celtics' success.

- C. Depth and Experience: The Celtics boast a well-rounded roster with veterans like Marcus Smart and Al Horford providing leadership and experience. The addition of Damian Lillard further bolsters their offensive firepower and creates a potent scoring threat from multiple positions.

D. Defensive Prowess: Coach Mazzulla emphasizes defensive discipline and communication, resulting in a highly effective unit. Players like Robert Williams III and Smart are defensive anchors who can shut down opposing offenses.

Weaknesses.

A. Reliance on Key Players: The Celtics are heavily reliant on Tatum and Brown for scoring. While they are exceptional players, their fatigue or potential injuries would significantly impact the team's performance.

B. Lack of Size: The Celtics could struggle against teams with strong interior presences. Their rebounding and ability to defend the paint might be tested in playoff matchups against teams with dominant big men.

C. Potential for Complacency: The Celtics have established themselves as a top contender in the East. However, complacency could set in, impacting their motivation and desire to push themselves further.

2. *Milwaukee Bucks*

Strengths.

A. Giannis Antetokounmpo: The reigning Finals MVP, Giannis Antetokounmpo, remains a dominant force. His combination of size, strength, and athleticism makes him virtually unstoppable around the rim.

B. Jrue Holiday's Two-Way Play: Jrue Holiday provides invaluable contributions on both ends of the court. His elite defense and playmaking skills significantly elevate the Bucks' overall performance.

C. Khris Middleton's Scoring Threat: Khris Middleton is a reliable scorer who can create his own shot and knock down three-pointers. His presence alongside Giannis makes the Bucks' offense difficult to contain.

D. Experienced Team: The Bucks have a core of players who have been through the playoff gauntlet and know what it takes to succeed. Their experience and composure will be invaluable in high-pressure situations.

Weaknesses.

A. Ageing Core: The Bucks' championship core of Antetokounmpo, Holiday, and Middleton are all approaching the later stages of their careers. Their athleticism and stamina might decline over time, impacting their effectiveness.

B. Reliance on Giannis: The Bucks often rely heavily on Giannis to carry the offensive load. If teams manage to contain him effectively, their scoring options become limited.

C. Injury Concerns: Giannis and Middleton have both dealt with injuries in the past. Their health will be crucial to the Bucks' success in the playoffs.

3. *Other Eastern Conference Threats*

While the Celtics and Bucks stand as the frontrunners in the Eastern Conference, other teams possess the potential to make a deep playoff run.

- Philadelphia 76ers: Joel Embiid's dominance inside and the return of Ben Simmons create a formidable inside-outside duo. However, their success hinges on improved perimeter shooting and a more cohesive team identity.

- Miami Heat: The Heat are renowned for their defensive prowess and veteran leadership. Jimmy Butler's competitive spirit and Kyle Lowry's playmaking abilities make them a difficult matchup for any team.

- Cleveland Cavaliers: Darius Garland and Jarrett Allen have formed a dynamic young core, and the return of Evan Mobley provides additional defensive strength. Their youth and energy could pose a challenge to established contenders.

As the playoffs unfold, it will be fascinating to witness how these strengths and weaknesses play out, ultimately revealing the team with the grit, talent, and determination to reign supreme in the Eastern Conference.

Chapter 3: Western Conference Contenders

The Western Conference of the NBA is a veritable battlefield, where elite teams clash in an epic struggle for dominance. Each season, a new chapter unfolds in this ongoing rivalry, with established contenders vying for supremacy alongside rising stars and hungry newcomers. As we turn our attention to the West, let's delve into the top contenders poised to make a deep playoff run.

1. Denver Nuggets

Strengths.

- A. Nikola Jokic's MVP-caliber Play: Nikola Jokic, the reigning MVP, is arguably the most dominant player in the league. His exceptional passing skills, basketball IQ, and ability to score inside and out make him virtually unguardable.

- B. Healthy Murray and Porter Jr.: The return of Jamal Murray and Michael Porter Jr. adds significant firepower to the Nuggets' offense. Their scoring ability and offensive versatility take pressure off Jokic and create a more dynamic scoring attack.

- C. Strong Supporting Cast: Aaron Gordon has emerged as a key contributor on both ends of the court, providing much-needed defense and athleticism. Kentavious Caldwell-Pope's perimeter shooting adds another dimension to their offense.

D. Depth and Versatility: The Nuggets boast a deep roster with players who can contribute in various ways. Their ability to adjust their game plans and adapt to different opponents makes them a difficult matchup.

Weaknesses.

A. Inexperienced Backcourt: While Murray and Porter Jr. are talented players, they lack extensive playoff experience. This could potentially impact their performance under pressure in crucial games.

B. Potential Defensive Struggles: The Nuggets' perimeter defense could be tested against elite offenses. They might struggle to contain teams with strong guard play and perimeter shooting.

C. Reliance on Jokic: While Jokic is a dominant player, the Nuggets could become overly reliant on him, especially if other players struggle offensively.

2. Phoenix Suns

Strengths.

A. Devin Booker's Scoring Prowess: Devin Booker is a prolific scorer who can create his own shot and knock down three-pointers with ease. His offensive firepower makes him a nightmare for opposing defenses.

B. Chris Paul's Leadership and Playmaking: Chris Paul, despite his age, remains a phenomenal point guard. His leadership, playmaking skills, and clutch shooting are invaluable assets to the Suns.

C. Deandre Ayton's Dominance: Deandre Ayton has developed into a dominant force in the paint. His rebounding, scoring, and defensive presence anchor the Suns' inside game.

D. Strong Team Culture: The Suns have built a strong team culture under Coach Monty Williams. Their chemistry, communication, and on-court camaraderie contribute to their success.

Weaknesses.

A. Ageing Chris Paul: Chris Paul's age and injury history remain concerns. Any decline in his performance could significantly impact the Suns' championship aspirations.

B. Reliance on Booker: The Suns often rely heavily on Booker for scoring. If teams manage to contain him effectively, their offensive options become limited.

C. Lack of Size in the Frontcourt: The Suns lack a dominant big man alongside Ayton. This could be exploited by teams with strong interior presences.

3. Other Western Conference Threats

While the Denver Nuggets and Phoenix Suns are considered the top contenders in the West, other teams possess the potential to disrupt the established order.

- Golden State Warriors: Stephen Curry and Draymond Green remain a formidable duo, and the addition of Andrew Wiggins provides another scoring threat. However, their aging core and recent injuries raise questions about their sustainability.

- Los Angeles Clippers: Kawhi Leonard's return alongside Paul George makes the Clippers a significant threat. Their depth, talent, and experience make them a potential force in the playoffs.

- Los Angeles Lakers: LeBron James' leadership and Anthony Davis' dominance inside make the Lakers a dangerous team. However, their recent struggles and roster issues cast doubt on their ability to make a deep playoff run.

The Western Conference is a crucible where only the most resilient and talented teams emerge victorious. As the playoffs approach, the intensity of competition will escalate, showcasing the pinnacle of basketball talent and strategic brilliance. The battle for the West promises to be a thrilling spectacle, with each team vying for a chance to represent the conference in the NBA Finals. Only time will reveal which team will rise above the rest and claim ultimate glory.

Chapter 4: Predicting the Conference Finals

With the regular season drawing to a close and playoff berths secured, the focus shifts towards the ultimate showdown: the NBA Finals. However, before the championship clash unfolds, two crucial battles must be fought - the Conference Finals in both the East and West. These contests represent the culmination of months of hard work and dedication, with each team vying for the right to represent their conference on the grandest stage.

Eastern Conference Finals Projected Matchup: Boston Celtics vs. Milwaukee Bucks

Reasoning.
- The Celtics and Bucks have emerged as the frontrunners in the East throughout the regular season. Their consistent performance, strong core players, and championship experience make them the most likely contenders to face off in the Conference Finals.

Key Factors to Consider.
- Jayson Tatum vs. Giannis Antetokounmpo: This matchup between two MVP-caliber players will be pivotal. Tatum's offensive prowess will be tested against Giannis' defensive dominance.

- Team Depth and Experience: Both teams boast deep rosters with experienced players who have played in high-pressure situations. The ability to contribute from different players and withstand injuries will be crucial.

- Coaching Strategies: Joe Mazzulla's tactical adjustments and Mike Budenholzer's defensive schemes will be put to the ultimate test. The team that can make the best in-game adjustments will gain a significant advantage.

- Prediction: This series promises to be a close and hard-fought battle. Ultimately, the Boston Celtics' superior offensive firepower and depth are expected to edge out the Milwaukee Bucks, propelling them to the Eastern Conference championship and a chance to compete in the NBA Finals.

Western Conference Finals Projected Matchup: Denver Nuggets vs. Phoenix Suns

Reasoning.
- The Denver Nuggets and Phoenix Suns have consistently ranked among the top teams in the West. Their dynamic offenses, dominant players, and strong team cultures make them the favorites to clash in the Western Conference Finals.

Key Factors to Consider.

- Nikola Jokic vs. Deandre Ayton: This battle between two elite big men will be fascinating. Jokic's passing skills and versatility will be challenged by Ayton's defensive presence and rebounding prowess.

- Backcourt Dynamics: The Nuggets' backcourt of Jamal Murray and Michael Porter Jr. will face a tough test against the veteran leadership of Chris Paul and Devin Booker. The team that can control the tempo and dictate the pace of the game will gain the upper hand.

- Coaching Adjustments: Coach Michael Malone's ability to adapt his strategies to counter the Suns' defensive schemes will be crucial. Monty Williams' experience and leadership will be invaluable assets for Phoenix.

- Prediction: This series is expected to be a high-scoring, fast-paced affair. The Denver Nuggets' well-rounded offensive attack and Nikola Jokic's MVP-caliber play are expected to be the difference-makers, propelling them to the Western Conference championship and a chance to compete in the NBA Finals.

The Conference Finals will showcase the culmination of months of preparation and competition. With the pressure mounting and the stakes at an all-time high, these series are guaranteed to provide thrilling basketball action and drama. Only the most resilient and talented teams will emerge victorious, earning the coveted opportunity to compete for the ultimate prize: the NBA championship.

Next Chapter: In Chapter 5, we will delve into the highly anticipated NBA Finals, analyzing the strengths and weaknesses of each team and predicting the ultimate champion.

Chapter 5: NBA Finals Showdown

The Pinnacle of Basketball: Predicting the NBA Finals Champion

The NBA Finals represent the pinnacle of basketball achievement. After months of intense competition, two teams remain standing, vying for the ultimate glory: the NBA championship. This stage demands not only exceptional talent and physical prowess but also a mental fortitude to withstand the immense pressure and perform under the brightest lights.

Projected Matchup: Boston Celtics vs. Denver Nuggets

Reasoning.
- Based on the analysis presented in Chapters 2 and 3, the Boston Celtics and Denver Nuggets are projected to emerge victorious from their respective Conference Finals, setting the stage for an epic showdown in the NBA Finals.

Key Matchups and Factors to Consider.
- Jayson Tatum vs. Nikola Jokic: This individual matchup is likely to be the focal point of the series. Tatum's explosive scoring will be tested against Jokic's elite defensive capabilities and passing skills.

Strength vs. Versatility.
- The Celtics possess a strong and experienced core, while the Nuggets boast a more versatile and dynamic offense. The team

that can best exploit the other's weaknesses will gain a significant advantage.

Coaching Strategies.
- Joe Mazzulla's tactical adjustments will need to counter Michael Malone's offensive schemes. Both coaches will need to adapt their strategies throughout the series to keep the other team guessing.

Home Court Advantage.
- The Celtics are expected to have home court advantage throughout the series, potentially giving them a psychological edge and the support of their passionate fanbase.

Team Chemistry and Experience.
- Both teams possess strong team chemistry and experienced players who have played in high-pressure situations. The team that can maintain its composure and execute under pressure will be more likely to succeed.

Prediction.
- The 2024 NBA Finals are anticipated to be a highly competitive series, going down to the wire. However, the Boston Celtics' strong defense, experienced core, and home court advantage are expected to be the deciding factors. Their ability to contain Nikola Jokic and force turnovers will be crucial to their success. Ultimately, the Celtics are predicted to overcome the Denver Nuggets in a close-fought series, capturing their 18th NBA

championship and solidifying their place among the league's dynasties.

While the prediction favors the Boston Celtics, unforeseen circumstances can significantly impact the outcome of the series. Injuries, unexpected upsets, and individual player performances can all play a role in determining the ultimate victor. Therefore, it's important to consider various scenarios.

1. Injury to Key Players.

   Injuries to key players like Jayson Tatum or Nikola Jokic could drastically alter the landscape of the series. The team that can adapt to such adversity and rely on its depth will be better prepared to overcome such challenges.

2. Team Adjustments and Strategies.

   Both teams will have ample time to analyze each other's strengths and weaknesses throughout the series. Their ability to adjust their strategies, exploit weaknesses, and identify mismatches will be critical to their success.

3. Unsung Heroes and Individual Performances.

   Sometimes, unexpected players can step up and become heroes in the NBA Finals. The team that benefits from such individual performances could gain a significant advantage and steal a crucial game.

While predictions provide a framework and analysis, the true beauty of the NBA Finals lies in its inherent unpredictability. The unexpected often unfolds, creating thrilling moments and defying expectations. By embracing the potential for surprises and upsets, fans can appreciate the drama and suspense that make the NBA Finals truly captivating.

Next Chapter: In Chapter 6, we will summarize the key points of the analysis, acknowledge its limitations, and encourage readers to embrace the excitement and anticipation surrounding the NBA playoffs.

Chapter 6: Conclusion and Disclaimers

As we conclude this analysis of the 2024 NBA Playoffs, it's crucial to acknowledge the limitations of predictions and embrace the inherent unpredictability of the sport. While we have meticulously analyzed team strengths, weaknesses, and potential playoff scenarios, unforeseen circumstances like injuries, individual performances, and coaching strategies can significantly impact the outcome.

Key Points of the Analysis

- The Boston Celtics and Denver Nuggets are predicted to emerge victorious from their respective Conference Finals and face off in the NBA Finals.

- The Celtics' strong defense, experienced core, and home court advantage are expected to be decisive factors in their favor.

- The Nuggets' dynamic offense, led by Nikola Jokic, presents a significant challenge to the Celtics' defensive scheme.

- The series is anticipated to be close and competitive, with the potential for upsets and unexpected individual heroics.

Limitations of Predictions

- Injuries to key players can drastically alter the course of the playoffs.

- Teams may adjust their strategies and tactics throughout the series, making predictions less reliable.

- Unexpected individual performances and team chemistry can significantly impact the outcome.

The beauty of the NBA playoffs lies precisely in its unpredictable nature. The unexpected often unfolds, creating thrilling moments and defying expectations. By embracing the possibility of surprises and upsets, we can fully appreciate the drama and suspense that make the playoffs so captivating.

Regardless of the outcome, the NBA playoffs offer a spectacle of athleticism, talent, and strategic brilliance. It's a time to celebrate the passion of the players, the dedication of the fans, and the incredible journey that unfolds on the basketball court. So, let us enjoy the excitement and anticipation that the playoffs bring, knowing that regardless of the final score, we are witnessing a testament to the power and beauty of the sport.

Thank you for joining me on this journey through the analysis of the 2024 NBA Playoffs. May the best team win, and may the games be a testament to the incredible talent and passion that define the sport.

Chapter 7: A Legacy Forged in Hardwood

From humble beginnings in a New York City YMCA to its present status as a global phenomenon, the National Basketball Association (NBA) has carved a remarkable path through history. This journey, spanning over seven decades, is a testament to the enduring power of sport, the evolution of athleticism, and the unwavering passion of players and fans alike.

The Early Days

The NBA's roots can be traced back to 1946, when the Basketball Association of America (BAA) was formed. This fledgling league consisted of eleven teams primarily located in the Northeast and Midwest. The early years were marked by financial struggles, limited media coverage, and intense competition with rival leagues. However, the BAA laid the foundation for the future, showcasing the raw talent of pioneers like George Mikan and Joe Fulks.

Merger and Expansion

In 1949, the BAA merged with its competitor, the National Basketball League (NBL), to form the National Basketball Association. This merger marked a significant turning point, consolidating talent and resources, and paving the way for the league's growth. Over the next two decades, the NBA experienced a period of dramatic expansion, welcoming new teams across the country and embracing the diverse talent pool of America. Legends like Bill Russell, Wilt Chamberlain, and Oscar Robertson emerged, captivating the nation with their incredible athleticism and competitive spirit.'

The Golden Age

The 1980s ushered in a golden age for the NBA, characterized by iconic rivalries, global expansion, and the rise of charismatic superstars. Magic Johnson and Larry Bird reignited the Celtics-Lakers rivalry, thrilling fans with their contrasting styles and captivating personalities. Michael Jordan, with his unparalleled skill and insatiable drive, redefined the game and became a global icon, transcending sport and influencing popular culture. The NBA, fueled by this star power, expanded its reach internationally, establishing a fan base that stretched far beyond the borders of the United States.

Modern Era and Innovation

The modern era of the NBA has been marked by technological advancements, changing demographics, and the emergence of new basketball philosophies. Teams have embraced analytics, optimizing strategies and maximizing player potential. Players like LeBron James, Stephen Curry, and Kevin Durant have rewritten the record books and pushed the boundaries of athleticism. The league has also seen increased diversity, with international players like Dirk Nowitzki, Yao Ming, and Giannis Antetokounmpo leaving their mark on the game.

A Legacy of Inspiration

Today, the NBA stands as a global powerhouse, entertaining millions of fans across the world. It has provided a platform for athletes to showcase their talents, inspire generations of youth, and promote social change. From the early days of George Mikan to the current era of superstars like

Giannis Antetokounmpo and Stephen Curry, the NBA's legacy is one of resilience, innovation, and a shared love for the game.

Looking Ahead

As the NBA enters its eighth decade, the future looks bright. The league continues to evolve, embracing new technologies, engaging with fans in innovative ways, and expanding its reach into new markets. With a commitment to inclusivity, social responsibility, and exciting on-court action, the NBA promises to remain a cultural touchstone, captivating audiences and inspiring future generations for years to come.

www.ingramcontent.com/pod-product-compliance
Lightning Source LLC
Chambersburg PA
CBHW071325080526
44587CB00018B/3352